CRABS

and Other Poems

By Vanessa Runs

DEDICATION

For my family

TABLE OF CONTENTS

AFTERNOON WELL WASTED

Create and consume

Create and consume

Create and consume

This is the way of the Gods

Troubles float through the air and attach themselves to the land and the people

But under the water and in my dreams I am free

ARTIST

I didn't know you were an artist, dear

You've been hiding indoors

Making all your own toys

Hammering away

Lost in a holy cave

But now that I can see you out here in the light

I can tell that you are an Artist

And that nobody must question your way

Is that a microphone on your banjo?

Are those real trees growing out of your head?

Exactly how many cats do you have in there?

ALTARS

I want

Peace for my soul

Harmony for my spirit

Holiness for my tongue

I am a tree farmer

I am a healer

I am sharpening my tools

Dear heart,

Listen to me closely

Go build altars

Everywhere you go

AGING

I have no lines on my face to betray my age

The only thing that betrays me is the experience of a full life

To get me high and talking about what I've done and seen

All the things I've eaten and studied

All the places I've been and the people I've met

And you slowly start to piece it together

That I must be very old

BROWN

I do what I want

I say what I want

I dress how I want

I think what I want

I be what I am

I am an old redwood with roots deep through time and culture

Just plain brown and blending in

BLIND

When I heard there was a blind man in my family

I went to that man's home and I lived in his backyard

I danced under his window while he was asleep and all the spirits said,

"What a waste! Such a beautiful thing Dancing in the darkness

For a blind man while he is asleep!"

And they all complained to God about this horrid injustice

And that is how everyone in my family

Came to receive clear sight

BEAUTY 1

Beauty is my compass

An evil man has no need for beauty but a poor man pays his debts with it

My smile might forsake me but beauty never will

Did you know that every culture values beauty?

So go ahead and travel everywhere

If a flower blooms only among other flowers

How will she know how beautiful she is?

BEAUTY 2

Sometimes the joy is so deep that my expression is to create beautiful things

Sometimes the pain is so harsh that my medicine is to create beautiful things

And so is the way with beauty

Good or bad

Rich or poor

Fat or hungry

She never leaves your side

BEAUTY 3

Value beauty over modesty

Beauty carries thought and design and intention

There is a holiness in that

I am a sand mandala to your eyes and mine

I am of my own design

What's the point of being alive

If not to be surrounded by beautiful things?

Goodness is easy to fake

But true beauty cannot be hidden

BEAUTY 4

Calling on the peaceful: Let there be peace

Calling on the authentic: Let there be transparency

Calling on the brave: Let there be courage

Calling on the dreamers: Let there be hope

Calling on the worshippers: Let there be honor

Calling on the compassionate: Let there be empathy

Calling on the ancient: Let there be a remembering

Calling on myself: Let there be beauty

BOOK ARE TEACHERS THAT LIVE LONGER

Sometimes my words seem so important

That I feel I have to get them all out in a rush

But then I remember that these words have been spoken before

The message is already out there

And that makes me sad

To think that despite the good word, there still has been no change

Too many of us are still struggling and suffering too much

But then I remember

That my words today are not for right now

But for ones to read who are not yet here

Do not focus on the ones who are not, child

Keep looking to the ones who will be

They will be out there looking for you

Someday but not today

The ones who need you
Will see you in time

BECOME ACCUSTOMED TO CHANGE

Because by the time you figure things out

You're old

And you have to learn new things that didn't exist before

CRABS

The best thing you can do for the world is to go outside and be your true self

Once those people have seen you, move out further so that new people can see you

Then travel to far away places until you have been seen in all the public spaces

And plant the seed of yourself in little gardens that you allow to grow wild wherever you go

So those who are coming behind you can follow your path and say things like:

I didn't realize there was another one just like me!

That's how you find community and family: by letting your light shine

But if you hide your light

You can still be an ecosystem onto yourself

Because you are a Universe of One

And maybe you can feed the birds

Because some adults are afraid of birds and some children chase them

But you would probably enjoy them

Birds are a community of their own and they can become your family

Everyone should have a living family of some kind

If you don't have family and you don't want to feed the birds, just go to the ocean

There are billions of crabs there, just running all over the rocks for free

They can be your family

I have been hanging out with these guys for years, so it will be the two of us plus crabs

I think we can get a real ecosystem going

See you on the low tide, my love

CRABS 2

Not everything can be known by poetry

For example, how could I explain my crab dance?

If I could show you, you could use it freely for yourself, as needed

I can only imagine all the crabby situations you would get yourself in

This is how I look when I dance:

Sometimes I am ripping abs of steel

Other times I am rubbing my Buddha belly and smiling like a cat

Everything in creation is a dance

If you cannot believe this

Then you do not know God

CHARACTER

I want character in my face

I want to weave a story with weathered skin

I want expressions deep with river lines

I want ocean scars speckling my tired body

When I am old

For now, I'll have fresh skin

Fly away hair and no wrinkles

Just a baby pushing out of her shell

Screaming at the world:

WHAT'S TO EAT?

DOVES

My gurus gather under my window and bless me everyday:

May all your sounds be beautiful ones

May those who know you call you love

May your presence carry peace

DEAR SUN

Every day you honor me with your visit

You are constant

You are consistent

You are here again

Your rays bring me energy and opportunity

Your light fills my home

Your heat gives me power

Why should I not bow to you?

Why should I not become your disciple?

DISTURBANCE OF THOUGHT

You might as well stop chasing the ravens

I am feeding them behind your back

I am a thorn in your flesh

I am good at this

So step aside my friend and enjoy the show

Am I a missionary or a magician?

Sometimes it's hard to tell

I am Myself

And all the Teachers who have come before me

And Now

I know more than the teacher

So I am New God

EVIL

When evil comes around I will step boldly out: a child playing with a baby

To stop evil in its surprised tracks just long enough for my kittens to pounce

Go ahead and laugh if you want

Cuteness is a weapon too

FERTILE

There is a garden growing in my soul

My roots are: observation and experience

It is better to learn from the mistakes of others than to commit your own

My fruits are: peace and acceptance

Within myself and also within my family

My seeds are: this poem and the songs I sing

I sprinkle myself everywhere I go

FEAR

Oh Fear!

It is you again!

You scared me.

How have you been?

I see you are hungry.

So am I.

FAMILY

I was born into a family of sweet sisters and beautiful mothers

I have been assimilated into a tribe of wild artists and holy vagabonds

I will build a family of brave warriors and powerful propagators

Let our holy words not be translated

Let them be spoken in our native tongues

Created by our own minds and hearts

And carried by our own voices on windy days

I am an echo of the voices who have come before me

With the same message from the same soul:

We must love ourselves first

We must love ourselves first

We must love ourselves first

FREEDOM

I want freedom:

Of movement

Of play

Of love

Of spirit

Of joy

Of soul

Of thought

Of choice

From need

From worry

From want

From fear

I want to build my home in peace

In harmony and synchronicity and close proximity to those

I love

I want to be my true self with my family in a beautiful and simple space

Where I am free to learn, practice, teach and observe

I seek self-control and mastery:

Of thought

Of word

Of emotion

To communicate non-violently with anyone in any language

To listen

To fearlessly share of myself

For us all I wish empathy and compassion

Over indifference and complacency

Equinamity over division

Truth instead of lies

And Love instead of fear

FAITH

I am a whirling dervish

I can twirl for three days straight

In the ark of Noah, I leave off swimming

To the dog park, I bring cats

FIRE

Think of your problems as tracing paper

Thin and delicate and translucent

Think of me as your forest fire

I flash through your front door

I do not discriminate or show favoritism

I can only consume and destroy

FULL MOON 1

The moon swung low and blessed me last night
She licked my face and said:
Anything you ask, you will have it

I replied:
If you have blessed me
Then make me a blessing too

Let my feet bless the ground they tread
Let my hands bless the life they touch
Let my tongue bless every soul that hears me sing
Let blessing shed from my body
The way that hair sheds from my head

Let fertile seeds fall to the ground below me
As I pass
The way that old skin falls to the ground

Then Moon swept me up in her arms

And we danced into the night

FULL MOON 2

God is drunk again and out of control

Stumbling through the stars and spitting on me when she speaks

Let's shed our clothes for a minute and dance together under this moonlight

Have you ever heard a woman giggle until sunrise?

Why are you pretending to scowl when your heart is laughing?

Why are you trying to walk when you really mean to run?

Why are you wearing that coat when your skin underneath is so beautiful?

GOOD MORNING

Where is the sun rising today?

Where is the sun setting today?

Where will my freshwater be coming from?

Where will my greywater be coming from?

Have my pets and family been fed?

Where's the coffee?

GOODNESS

Be careful of goodness

When it enters your life

It will consume you

You will not be able to stop thinking about doing good

One day you will paint your nails and say to your hands

Hands! I have just painted you!

You are not allowed to do good for five minutes!

But your hands will still do good and you will ruin your nails

Beware of that day

If you become given to goodness

Don't say I didn't warn you

Doing good is a gateway habit, even if you begin with poor intentions

Even if your works are silly and misguided at first

If you ever get the chance

Become the best at goodness

GOOD WORDS

Dear sweet child

Take me where you go

Show me where you sleep

Tell me of the animals you love

And the trees that you value

Let me love you without shame

Let me hold you without hesitation

Today,

Be me for a while

And I will be you

Precious one

Things are really tough right now

I know it's easy to feel alone

But we are not alone

In joy, we see darkness with new eyes

Be patient and forgiving like the tree

If you need me, call my name

My ears are tuned to your voice

There is no better way to heal than together

I love you

GRATITUDE

What was your last meal?

Who served it to you?

Did you eat alone, or did you have family by your side?

Now eat your next meal in compassion and understanding

If your belly is full of food, why should you not feel inspired

To feed and nourish the hungry around you?

Strengthen your commitment

To keep a light on for the lonely

A meal out for the hungry

A song for the hopeless

That surround you every day

Leave a bowl of water out for whoever might need it

Spread a little seed for the native birds

Bring an extra blanket for whoever might be cold

Offer eye contact to anyone who might be feeling invisible

All you say and do has an impact
On more than you can know or understand

Show joy in your daily life
Dance while you cook
Sing while you poop

Plants are listening
Birds are watching

GRACE

Grace came to me
At the last second
In the final tunnel
At the darkest hour

Grace found me
And broke me
And murdered me
And left me here in a lump
Of saggy love
And leaky joy
And dripping peace

Who am I?

I am not me
I am a symbol
I am a hope

I am a totem

I am a holy and wild creature
I am beauty for the sake of beauty

When I look up, I see myself
When I look within, I see God
Nothing divine is alien to me

Understanding
Wisdom
Ancient Truths
The things that are not heard
The things that are not seen
Let them come to me
With a wild side of joy

I am blinded by love
I don't know how or why
I dance in the darkness
Where nobody can see

I am nobody and I am new here

I know nothing and I am everything

I am The Universe, extending a helpful hand

I am The Love you never expected

I am The Friend in the final hour

I am the Mother and Father who were there all along

I am the Sister and the Brother, your very own blood

I am gratitude

I am gratitude

I am gratitude

GRIEF

I carry grief in a bottle around my neck

I carry grief as an anchor around my legs

I carry grief

And grief carries me

GHETTO

The good thing about growing up poor

Is that money becomes an unreliable source of happiness from an early age

You learn how to feel good with earth, fire, water, and air

Beautiful thoughts can replace food

If you are young enough

HUMAN 1

You are human because of your potential for art and music and magic

Because you can create beautiful things to enchant and intrigue

And also your ability to manipulate your environment with your thumbs

If you are not busy being a great artist, perhaps you can fill a bowl with fresh water and place it outside for any birds in need today

Such a simple act as this is fully human and redeems you in every way

Kindness to birds is the most beautiful way to be human

HUMAN 2

I am human

I walk out into the world with the earth beneath my feet

I see with my eyes

I listen with my ears

I think on what needs to be done and then I do it.

I do what is right no matter what is popular

I do what is right no matter what is legal

I do what is right no matter what it costs me

I leave notes for the ones who have not yet arrived

Who might also be trying to do right

Who might also know how to read

Who might be human too

HOW TO PLEASE GOD

Keep your mind on divinity alone

On kindness, compassion, unity and peace

Practice patient thought

Have humility wash over your mind and absorb your intellect

Make compassion your goal

Practice physical movement to express joy

And to honor what is holy within your own body

Give your works over to goodness

Set your hands to holy action

Act the acts of love

When everyone else is afraid to act

Finally

Behave with self control

Master your thoughts

Master your movements

Master your actions

Control your emotions

Control your mind

Then move freely among all things

Move beautifully

Move gracefully

And dance

Dance

Dance

Never stop dancing

HOLY FRIDAY

Wake up

Open your eyes

Smile

Open your heart

Open your ears

Listen

Who is around you?

What do you see?

Find life

See the human

See the animals

See the plants

See yourself

Think on what all those living things need

Today

To feel safe and loved

Then set your hands to work

Set your feet to dancing

Set your heart to hoping

And set your voice to singing

HARBOR SEAL PUP

Good morning world!

Hello sand and surf!

What's going on around me?

What's there to sniff?

Hello are you my mum?

HATRED

We will not share your hate

We will not taste your anger

We will not give away this piece in our hearts

You cannot steal it

It is our birthright

I have set my felines on your scent

Do not come back

You are not welcome in my home

You are not welcome in my heart

HEATHEN

I had to take up smoking and drinking and cursing and nudity

Just to set myself apart from you

Because you called yourself holy while you were doing evil

So I burned my robes and cut my hair just to be different

I was born pure but now I have altered myself

Because you claimed God while everything you did was a lie

Your curse is music to my ears

Because it means I am nothing like you

I thought those bad habits would be a gateway to evil

But it only made me see more of the Beauty

Because God was inside me that whole time

And I don't think you know Us at all

HUSBAND

My husband said he didn't believe I could cook and so I showed him how I could

Then he said he didn't believe I could sew

So I did, just to show him

I'm starting to see how it's very easy

To get me to do things

HIJAB

I am in love with a girl in a hijab
My buddy asked me,
How do you know you like her?
If you haven't seen her whole head?

I know from the kindness in her eyes
I know from the softness of her hands
I know from the truth on her tongue

HOLY RAMEN

Dear limp noodle

You have fed more starving students

Than the Pope

To the impoverished,

You have given more comfort

Than the saints

You have inspired more hope

Than religion

Oh Holy Ramen

Reviver of hearts

Heater of bones

You are food in my belly

You are water and noodle

You do not preach or ask for donations

You only nourish

HE SHE

I can see how one might confuse God for a man

A masculine strength is often needed

To appear this beautifully

This is my Mother

And my Father too

When a woman's hand is needed, a Woman will do the work

When a man's hand is needed, a Woman might be doing that too

I AM THE GOD

Your God is a scientist and you are his experiment

Like you, there are many others

That's why he doesn't care about your daily thoughts

But I am the God who walks among you

Who anticipates your needs and movements

Who actually cares what happens in your daily life

I am the God that loves you

I HAVE

Have you ever been kissed by God and been so embarrassed someone might see

So you rub your face with the river Kern before anyone notices?

Have you ever sung so beautifully into the wind then looked around, expecting to see the trees dancing

But all that was there was a gentle drizzle?

Have you ever traveled so far in search of forbidden fruit but by the time you reached the ancient tree

All the fruit had rotted out and fallen to the ground

But you ate it anyway and it still worked?

Have you ever been in love with everything you ever saw especially your own sweet face

And your own strong body?

I AM SHITTING GOLD

I put this word here and I put that word there

And I put this word over here

Because it pleases me

I LOVE YOU

I love you no matter what you do

I love you no matter what you say

I love you no matter what you think

I love you no matter who you are

Love doesn't depend on who deserves what

Love only depends on me and who I am

It is a default state of the heart, no matter how much it is understood or ignored

What a treasure

To be loved so fully

To be seen so closely

To be held just right

I always save a spot for you in the parking spot next to mine

And God help the man who tries to park there

I cover that spot with birdseed so my pigeons will attack him

KNOWING

Nobody ever asks to taste God or to smell God

Everyone wants to see or hear

But smelling is how you really get to know a person

And nobody can ever know anyone without tasting them

KISSES

When I see your face

I do not see skin

I only see an obstacle

I must kiss through

LEARNING 1

How can I propagate plants and bees?

How can I communicate with an octopus in the wild?

How can I understand the moon and the tides?

What are the birds doing right now?

How can I create a musical sound that nobody has ever heard before?

How can I find my direction magnetically?

How can I grow food inside a moving vehicle?

How can I make my own clothes?

How can I promote peace and education?

What fish are in season right now?

How can I communicate with the trees that I grow from seed?

How can I bond with my cats?

How can I find privacy in California?

How can I plant and protect guerrilla urban sanctuary

gardens for insects and other small things?

How can I best serve the oceans of the planet?

How can I build and operate my own working printing press?

How can I meet a whale in the wild?

How can I build my own structures out of salvaged wood?

How can I create my own tinctures and potions and spells and totems?

How can I live near the ocean for the rest of my life?

How can I paint my memories with acrylic paint?

How far do my thoughts carry out into the universe?

How strong is my voice?

LEARNING 2

When I thought myself a learner, I prayed for teachers

Then Grief and Sorrow and Loss arrived at my door

They taught me Patience and Kindness and Compassion

They taught me Vulnerability and Faith and Resilience

I don't pray for teachers anymore

Now I just pray for cats

LILY

Be brave today

A flower shares its beauty freely, without seeking validation or payment

The sun herself is reward enough for beautiful creatures

Our efforts have not been in vain

We have not wasted a single second by sitting still

LOOKING AT MYSELF IN THE MIRROR

If I were to create a woman

Designed after my own heart

If I were to give her the life

She always wanted

If I were to feed her and water her

And give her everything she needed

No matter what others thought or said

If I were to vanquish her enemies

And prune from her life

All who might harm or silence or subdue her

This is what she would look like

This is who she would become

Here is the blessed face of the

Most Beautiful

Most Strongest

Most Perfect

Woman I know

See

Value

Treasure

Her

She is OCEAN TOTEM

She cannot be contained

She will never stop feeding

She is EARTH TOTEM

She will not be moved

Except by Her Own Wish

Or by Divine Command

She is FIRE TOTEM

All consuming and hungry

She has no respect for borders

The whole earth is Her Home

She is WIND TOTEM

You will hear her before you can see her

She is a savage howl from under the mountains

She lives at the root of every tree

She is SPIRIT TOTEM

You will never tame or imprison her

Her compassion is endless

Her kindness is infinite

Her art is transformational

Her work is Divine

She does not expect to be understood

She expects to be loved

And surrounded by simple beauties

What preciousness to my eyes

Is my own sweet face

May you also find yourself Living

In the Divine Breath

MAGIC

I am an exquisite creature

I hold the elements in my heart

I touch them

And test them

And turn them

I move things

I think things

I know things

I grow things

I am an exquisite creature

I am beautiful

I am powerful

I am magic

My fingers are magic

My toes are magic

My eyes are magic

Even my hair is magic

The way it grows like roots reaching

Towards the earth and also towards the sky

I do not require your worship, dear friend

But I do demand it

And I will use my magic in return

To worship you right back, my love

NO

Share your light, they said

But I will not

I will hoard my light

Until it is seeping moisture out of my pores

Until my cheeks are rosy and my teeth are white

Until I am timeless and ageless and everywhere

My thoughts of power will be mine

My thoughts of beauty will be mine

Feeding me first

Growing me first

From the inside out

Those who wish me out may lure me out

With moonlit serenades once a month

NEIGHBOURS

My neighbors are all birds and I am very kind to them

Thirteen doves coo peacefully at my window

I put water and seed out daily

The sparrow families are getting fat on my seed too

Some finches join the party

In the field, the killdeer run around chasing things

They build their homes on the ground

Every time a human goes by, they sound the alarm

Two ravens patrol the field and the surrounding buildings

I am also under their jurisdiction

Every time I put out something new, they come to
investigate

Other than two lizards, those are my neighbors

We're a quiet bunch.

If you ever get bored or sad

Thinking about the thoughts that you think about

Then maybe you can try thinking about birds instead.

OCEAN 1

If this is not my home, then I have no home

Even the pigeons know me here

If I cough, a human will startle

But the birds know where I am

Test and see

That those who love you will give you what you need

Even if they are animals

OCEAN 2

I came to the ocean with all of my struggles

I explained and complained

She whispered

Come closer child

I will rip your troubles dead

I came to the ocean with all my problems

I cried and I whined

She roared

Come closer child

I will see your struggles drowned

My ocean

My mother

My lover

My friend

I hope that someday it is said of me:

Her words helped me understand

The sacredness of Water

OCEAN 3

The ocean is a very boring place

Have you ever seen a manatee?

Those things are so boring

They float around all day and do nothing

Out of all the thousands of weddings that happen at the ocean

How many have ended in divorce?

Still the manatee floats in the same position he was in on the wedding day

Adults like to go to the ocean because it is a constant

It is a regulator

Nothing ever changes there

And their daily lives are filled with so much

Blah blah blah blah blah

That they come to the ocean to unwind

But for the traveling child

Who wants to swim to Hawaii

Who is hungry for life

The ocean is full of parents yelling

NOOO

COME BAAAACK

PUT YOUR CLOTHES BACK ON

The ocean can be a very boring place

For the Child

That's why I came as an Adult

To get naked

To dance in the waves

To do as I please

To say what I think

To be who I am

Sometimes children say,

See?

She's doing it

And we can be allowed to meet in the waves

OCEAN 4

Here on this blanket I sit

Just steps from the water

And I can come here with my blanket

Whether I am rich or poor

Brown or black

And nobody can drag me away

My father can't and neither can my mother

Because Ocean herself is my family and my friend

OCTOPUS 1

Octopus

Number Eight

You swim into my mind's eye

Siren

Magical creature

Monster of the sea

You are both hider and seeker

Learner and Teacher

Shifter and Sifter

Multi tasker

Cave dweller

I see you

Let us move through this planet without strain

Without blame or fault or greed

Let us regenerate while moving

In beauty

In grace

And again,

In beauty

OCTOPUS 2

When an octopus is placed inside a fishtank

It will sway with the currents of the ocean

Though the water does not move

In the same way,

We will sway to the beat of my own wild hearts

No matter what the climate

OH NO

My heart is starting to riot!

Here are my demands for myself in the next 24 hours:

Self-love

Self-understanding

Self-touch

Self-attention

Connect with family

Connect with natural and physical environment

Connect to gratitude

Eat well

Sleep well

Regulate temperature (hot, cold)

Create something new

Manage energy & set boundaries

Create/observe private solitudes, schedules, routines, rituals

Empower your physical body to move gracefully and efficiently in animal-worthy beauty, purity and joy

Connect to fun, creativity, and curiosity

Bathe your home in beautiful sound

PEACE 1

Peace is produced

When you love your whole self

When you care for your physical body

When you are not afraid of the darkness inside of you

When you live with integrity of mind and spirit and action

Blessed are the peacemakers

We do very well indeed

PEACE 2

Thirteen   doves   have   perched   themselves   outside   my
window

Better than ten thousand photos

Is one word that brings peace

I will not fight

I will lay down my God-given weapons

Even the ones that are words

Then I will sit down

And wait for you to join me

I sit for peace

I know peace

I think peace

I speak peace

I act peace

Peace In my heart

Peace In my home

Peace In my family

Peace In my community

Peace In my neighborhood

Peace In my city

Peace In my state

Peace in my province

Peace In my country

Peace across the globe

PEACE 3

Make a sound for peace

Starting Today

Right where you are

And I will make a sound from here

Until we can both of us hear each other

There are ways to communicate that transcend language barriers

They are:

Kindness

Compassion

Goodness

Joy

Gentleness

Humility

And Music

Become fluent in these languages

Then travel to a new place

PEACE 4

What a blessing to be able to sing your own song
Back into your own heart
At any time of the day or night
In any space you occupy

It's like catching your reflection in a glassy lake
Or finding yourself inside a different person
And falling in love

What a blessing to sing freely into the wind
In a place that I have made holy with my presence
To Myself in all my forms:

My ocean form
My bird form
My seal form
My dog form
My cat form

My crab form

And even my annoying human form

And not need to ask for payment because Payment has already been given in each breath

With every exhalation I am only re-gifting

What came to me freely

A lot of people express gratitude of movement and fitness

But I am overcome with gratitude of sound

What a blessing to create your own peace

PRAYER

I want all my thoughts to come mixed up with yours

I want all my actions to come mixed up with yours

I want all of my words to come out sounding just like your words

I want to stop needing food

I want to stop needing water

I want to stop needing clothing or shelter

I want to need only Your Love

And the sight of Your Face

Also, I want more animal company

Thank you for your time

PILGRIMAGE

It is very easy to be holy

If I go from the front of my vehicle to the back of my vehicle

That's a pilgrimage

Because my holy cats are always guarding the way with their sharp claws

A place is holy when I have arrived

Because I have arrived

And I am here now

PUPPIES

After all this time

After all this prayer

After all this devotion

I still have not seen my dreams realized

My dream is to lie down and have my body

Run over by puppies and kittens

And all of them will be mine

And I can take them all home

And nobody will say to me,

No you can't have them

Or something else ridiculous like,

You have to pick just one

POET

When I asked God to give me more poems

She giggled and gave me sight instead

Now everything I lay my eyes on

Becomes poetry in my mind

What a blessing to be a poet

It makes it okay to stay inside on a beautiful day

Just typing away

The secret is not in writing well

The secret is in thinking well

I finally made the calculations

I only have to live one bajillion more years

To finish writing all the things that haven't been said yet

And to finish re-writing all of the things that have been forgotten

POEM

A poem is something that reminds you of something that you should have known all along

But for some reason you didn't and nobody told you

And your life would have been way easier

If only you had seen that poem sooner

PROTECTION

Women who care for the earth: Do not fear

Women who care for animals: Do not hesitate

Women who grow food: Strengthen yourselves

Women who Listen: I am writing to you

Women of Wisdom: Find Me

I will cover you with my own body

I will fight your battles alongside

I will throw my voice to echo your own

I belong to you

We are family

We are sisters

We are nearly there

PAINTING

To know true brown, look into my skin

To know true pink, look into my ear

To know true love, look into my heart

PERFECTION

My dear, she asked me, What shall I wear for beauty?

I replied: If the matter is one of beauty, then you should wear nothing at all, my love

PROPEGATE

Good is the magician who fools his audience

Better is the magician who spills his secrets and creates new magicians

RELIEF

It all starts with a tiny entry point

Just a pin prick

And now comes the medicine

A cool rush

A gentle trickle

All my love from now on

Injected directly into your heart from mine

For as long as I am alive

RIVER

Life emerges from primordial waters

We are all made of water

Ebb

Bubble

Flow

Rush

There is no stopping us

There is no damming us

You have been flowing

You are flowing

You will continue to flow

Whatever stands in your path

You will move it over time

With the gentle and persistent nature of a water woman

Just like the raindrops fall from the sky

So will your obstacles

Drop away before you

Run in freedom, child

Run in force

Run in wild divinity

READING

When I was little my dad taught me to respect books by keeping them in good condition

So I folded the pages of my favorite parts and wrote little notes in the margins with my thoughts

Each book was a conversation where my comments carried equal weight

Or even a little more weight because I could write in color

The books weren't expecting me

They arched their backs and fluttered their wings

Trying all at once to propel their dusty ideas

Back into the path of a child

SILENCE 1

Is the lion silent as it stalks its prey?

Is the panther silent as it walks the earth?

Then I too can be respected

In my own wild silence

SILENCE 2

Nobody on earth has ever heard perfect silence

Even when you are silent I can still hear

The rustling of your feet

The shifting of your limbs

The beating of your heart

In silence I am reminded

Constantly

Constantly

How much I adore you

Sometimes when I am angry with you

I stop speaking

But that doesn't mean that I stopped loving you

I love you in silence

I love you in brilliance

I love you on this earth

SHHH

When I was angry, I yelled and hollered

But nobody paid attention

When I remained silent,

God himself tilted his head to hear me

SPIDER 1

You should know that you are part of my family

You should know that every spider is magical

You know also that we love each other

Communicator!

Oh, Wild One!

Weave your wishes into reality

Do not be afraid

This world can be a beautiful place for a spider

It can be a beautiful place for you too

I hope my dance can help you believe it

I am a simple brown spider spinning a web

I have come to you from a galaxy across the way

Let me in, babies

Let me crawl down your neck and whisper the Mystery into your brain

I love you so very much

SPIDER 2

I order my world

I sort my world

I clean my world

I eat my world

I consume my world

I destroy my world

I start over

SOCIETY

I made a mistake

Trying to fit in

Styling after your fashions

Mimicking your sounds

From now on I'll dress myself

With fabrics from my own land

The way my mother taught me

From now on I'll sing in my true voice

The timber of my father

Deep and Dark and Truth-telling

I will be shifting

I will be changing

I will be flighty

I will be moving

Like the dancing songbird that I am

SUNRISE

Take God in small doses and start young

That way if you get to be old, you will have built enough tolerance

To sit down some morning and share a cup of coffee with us

All that is left now to do is to enjoy

To experience joy in everything we do

And if my heart were ever to fill with sorrow again

That would be a sin against myself

Because the entire beauty of this world is wasted

When my eyes are full of tears

SIREN

I sit by the ocean and feel myself queen

A Fish among fish

A Woman among women

A God among Gods

And I know that my ways are my best ways

And my thoughts are my highest thoughts

And my space is my holiest place

I am holy because I baptized myself

I am perfect because I called myself perfect

It is finished because I said it was finished

Everything balanced and of my own design

My enlightenment is:

Do what you want

Eat what there is

When I see a family coming, I contort my body

I hold myself in the wildest positions

So every man woman and child can see plainly with their eyeballs for free

How a Woman might choose to move

Expertly in this skin shell

On both land and sea

I am a creature of the ocean and you are mostly water

Now you, too, belong to me

SMOKING

I'm going to keep smoking until I see God

I'm going to keep smoking until I am too lazy

To lift this divine pipe to my face

One

More

Time

I'm going to keep it hot

I'm going to keep it lit

I'm burning this fire every hour

Outside your window

The moon is the only thing that can silence me

The sun is the only thing that can outshine me

All I see is:

Glory

Glory

Glory

STAIN REMOVER

If you are ever worried about a small stain on your top

Or if your bangs are crooked

Or if you're not wearing shoes

Then simply smile

Because when you smile

Your face is so beautiful

Nobody will notice the stains

TRUCKER

There was once a trucker who prayed:

I love you so much, God

If you ever need a lift From LA to San Diego

Please let me be the one to drive you

The Man of God said to the trucker: You're an idiot

God has no need of your driving

Then they both died

Up in heaven God said to one of them:

Who are you?

And to the other he said:

Thanks for all the rides

TANTRUM

I hate everything except for trees
I hate adults and I hate children
I hate humans and I hate traffic
I hate urban sprawl and I hate concrete
I hate everything except for trees

I strip off my clothes and scream to God:
If you loved me
You would re-green my spaces
If you wanted to see me well
You would re-wild this rock

Send wind
Send fire
Send water
Send seeds
Send soil
There is digging to be done

In anger I gather up my sunflowers

On a sunny and beautiful day

And we all sit indoors together

In perfect silence

In the dark

Seen by no one

But even then

Even then

I can hear God laughing

UNITY

There are no cat people and there are no dog people

There are only animal lovers

All animals are basically the same

Once they can see that you love them

They tell you everything about themselves

VAGABOND

I was born with white paws but now they are brown
I have travelled so far and I have taken my shoes off

I have adorned myself with small birds
I have clothed myself with kittens

I came like a trickle but like an ocean I'll stay
Salty drops are all over my body

VOICE

I speak for myself

Because I am my own compass

And nobody deserves my voice

Or my love

Or my words

Or my time

More than I do

When I make a sound it will be deep and true

When I make a sound it will be eternal and wise

When I make a sound it will be guttural and resonating

My voice wakens the earth

And all the powers within me

That is why my tongue treads lightly

WHAT IF?

What if I don't have to do anything else?

What if everything I have done is already enough?

What if I just set myself free?

WORRIED

If I have flowers, I must worry about them wilting

If I have pets, I must worry about their health and wellbeing

In this way, surround yourself with the worries that you love to worry about

WISDOM

Who am I?

What is this power in me?

What have I become?

I pause

I think

I ask

How may I serve?

And now I listen

WHALE

Grandmother

You are Peaceful Strength

Emotional Rebirth

Keeper of history

Compassionate,

Solitary Creature

You glide between this world and the next

Let me ride on your back of wisdom

Let me heal against your textured skin

WORK

Your work is that thing you do

That makes you forget all other things

That makes time fly by

That makes nothing else matter

Work is not your burden

Work is your blessing

Work is your Personal Sacred Dance

On this earth

WORDY WOMAN

I collect sounds

I keep them deep in my throat, all the way down to my gut

Every sound I have ever made, I can make again

Including a whole lot of sounds that you have made

When the time is appropriate, I make the right sound

To elevate my family

Shall I say this again in Spanish or French?

WISDOM IS FREE FOR ME

If you ever doubt the existence of God, just look at this rose in my hair

It has been in there for weeks and it is still blooming

How can you explain it?

If you ever come to doubt the existence of God, let me tell you this story:

When I couldn't afford marijuana I had a tiny stash left

I was debating whether to smoke it now or save it for later

I decided to have faith that I would somehow get more weed

So I smoked it now

The next day, I noticed there was still a tiny bit left, so I had another hit

That evening I looked at my stash again

This is mostly stems, I thought

So I sifted my fingers through

And I found one more hit of wisdom

And so it has been, dear brothers

For three months now

And just like that one, I have other stories

Am I crazy or is somebody feeding me

From God's Personal Seed Pouch?

The birds and I are demanding to know

Show your face!

WOMAN IS MEDICINE

Her laughter is medicine

Her watchful presence is medicine

Her caring touch is medicine

May we never withhold this sacred healing

YOU DON'T NEED GOD

Instead of believing in God, why don't you just be God?

You're God from now on

Now he doesn't have to exist just in your imagination

Now God can be real, if you live like that truly

Instead of just through your tongue

YARD SALE

Where is God, they cry

But I'm right here and I've been here all along

I was just sitting inside my RV because I didn't see you had anything good to drink

So bring out your best things

Lay them out on your front yard so I can pick you out

Made in the USA
Columbia, SC
04 February 2023

11748956R00088